W9-COJ-908

CONNECTING CULTURES THROUGH FAMILY AND FOOD

The Middle Eastern Family Table

BY MARI RICH

CONNECTING CULTURES THROUGH FAMILY AND FOOD

The African Family Table

The Chinese Family Table

The Greek Family Table

The Indian Family Table

The Italian Family Table

The Japanese Family Table

The Mexican Family Table

The Middle Eastern Family Table

The Native American Family Table

The South American Family Table

The Thai Family Table

Connecting Cultures Through Family and Food

The Middle Eastern Family Table

By Mari Rich

MASON CREST

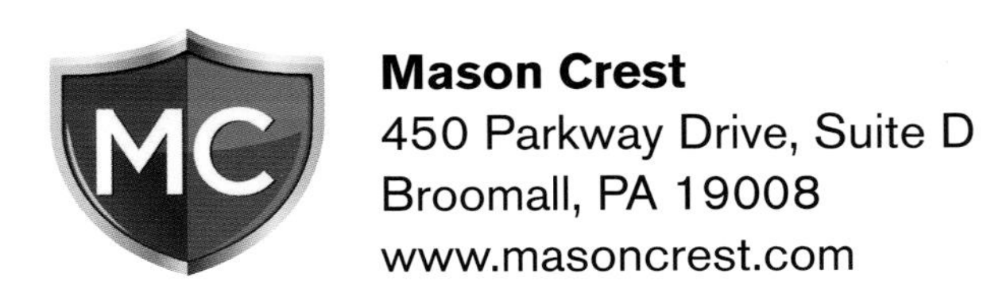

Mason Crest
450 Parkway Drive, Suite D
Broomall, PA 19008
www.masoncrest.com

Printed and bound in the United States of America.

First printing
9 8 7 6 5 4 3 2 1

Series ISBN: 978-1-4222-4041-0
Hardback ISBN: 978-1-4222-4049-6
EBook ISBN: 978-1-4222-7747-8

Produced by Shoreline Publishing Group LLC
Santa Barbara, California
Editorial Director: James Buckley Jr.
Designer: Tom Carling
Production: Patty Kelley
www.shorelinepublishing.com
Front cover: Shutterstock.com.

Library of Congress Cataloging-in-Publication Data
Names: Rich, Mari, author. Title: The Middle Eastern family table / by Mari Rich. Other titles: Connecting cultures through family and food.
Description: Broomall, PA : Mason Crest, 2018. | Series: Connecting cultures through family and food | Includes index.
Identifiers: LCCN 2017058186| ISBN 9781422240496 (hardback) | ISBN 9781422277478 (ebook)
Subjects: LCSH: Food habits--Middle East--Juvenile literature. | Cooking, Middle Eastern--Juvenile literature. | Middle Easterners--Food--Juvenile literature. | Middle East--Social life and customs--Juvenile literature. | Middle East--Emigration and immigration--Juvenile literature. | United States--Emigration and immigration--Juvenile literature.
Classification: LCC GT2853.M628 R53 2018 | DDC 394.1/20956--dc23 LC record available at https://lccn.loc.gov/2017058186

QR Codes disclaimer:

Contents

KEY ICONS TO LOOK FOR

Words to Understand: These words with their easy-to-understand definitions will increase the reader's understanding of the text, while building vocabulary skills.

Sidebars: This boxed material within the main text allows readers to build knowledge, gain insights, explore possibilities, and broaden their perspectives by weaving together additional information to provide realistic and holistic perspectives.

Educational Videos: Readers can view videos by scanning our QR codes, providing them with additional educational content to supplement the text. Examples include news coverage, moments in history, speeches, iconic moments, and much more!

Text-Dependent Questions: These questions send the reader back to the text for more careful attention to the evidence presented here.

Research Projects: Readers are pointed toward areas of further inquiry connected to each chapter. Suggestions are provided for projects that encourage deeper research and analysis.

Series Glossary of Key Terms: This back-of-the-book glossary contains terminology used throughout this series. Words found here increase the reader's ability to read and comprehend higher-level books and articles in this field.

Introduction

When people talk about the Middle East, they are not referring to a single country. The Middle East is a region that stretches from Africa in the west to the Arabian Gulf in the east. It contains more than 20 nations, including Algeria, Bahrain, Egypt, Iran, Israel, Jordan, Kuwait, Lebanon, Libya, Oman, Palestine, Qatar, Saudi Arabia, Syria, United Arab Emirates, and Yemen. You might think everyone in the Middle East is Muslim, but in fact, the region is home to people of a wide variety of faiths, including Christians, Jews, and Druze (members of an independent religion established in the 11th century).

Middle Easterners have immigrated to the United States since the late 19th century, and in the last few decades, their numbers have increased greatly. In 1970 there were about 200,000 Middle Eastern immigrants in the United States, but today, there are about 1.5 million, according to some estimates. California, Virginia, Texas, Michigan, and New York are among the US states with fast-growing numbers of people from the Middle East. People from the region have also settled in large numbers in Germany, France, the United Kingdom, and Russia.

People move from the Middle East for a number of reasons. Some are seeking greater educational and economic opportunities and a better life. Some are escaping persecution, violence, and strife in their native countries. Beginning in 2015, refugees trying to escape crises in places like

Afghanistan and Syria have contributed to what humanitarian groups called a massive shift of humanity unlike any ever seen before. (Of course, the flow is not just one way; there are many who have immigrated to the Middle East. In 1948, when the Jewish nation of Israel was established, people came from all over the world to live there. Many of these were Eastern European Jews who had survived the Holocaust and saw a chance to rebuild their lives. Jews from other countries still immigrate to Israel, in a process that is called making *aliyah*, which translates as "elevation" or "going up.")

Like all people from around the world who set out to find new homes, for whatever reason, Middle Easterners bring with them the families they love and the traditions that bind them together. Many of those traditions, as we will see, involve eating

Congregation Mickve Israel in Savannah, Georgia, was founded in 1733 by Jewish immigrants from Europe.

certain meals. Although a variety of countries make up the Middle East, most have favorite foods and flavors in common, including sesame seeds, figs and dates, yogurt, honey, olives and olive oil, chickpeas (also known as garbanzo beans in the West), mint, and pita bread. Certain cooking techniques (like placing meats on skewers to be grilled) are popular throughout the entire region, too.

Thanks to Middle Eastern immigrants, some of those foods and flavors have become mainstays in American cuisine in recent years. For example, you've probably seen a whole section of your supermarket's refrigerator case devoted to containers of hummus, a Middle Eastern dip made of chickpeas. Maybe the bread aisle features packages of pita for making sandwiches or individual pizzas.

Middle Easterners don't just introduce delicious new foods to foreign markets. They help make the countries where they move more diverse and interesting places.

Getting Here

"We were respected professionals when we lived in Egypt," Ahmed Maloof explains. "I taught high school, and my wife, Salwa, was a school counselor. Although things are very different for us here in New York, we don't

Words to Understand

Arab a member of the Arabic-speaking people

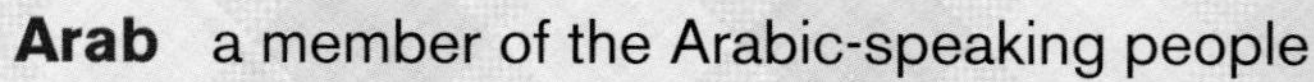

displaced forced to leave home, generally because of war, persecution, or natural disaster

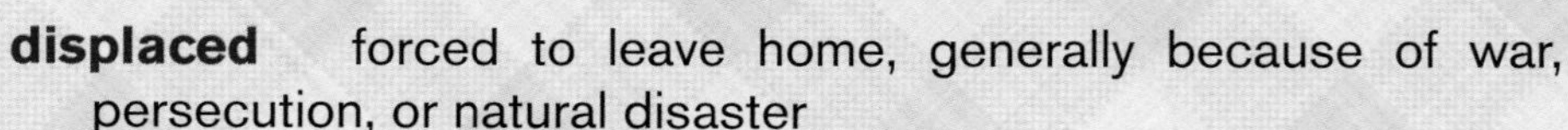

emissary a person sent on a special mission

literate able to read and write

Ottoman Empire an empire created by Turkish tribes that lasted more than 600 years. At its peak, it controlled large portions of the Middle East, including what is now Syria, Israel, and Egypt, as well as most of southeastern Europe and other places.

peddler a person who sells goods from a mobile site, such as a cart or truck

persecution criticism, danger, or threats made against a person due to their religious or ethnic background

The Middle East is filled with different countries and cultures, but most people who emigrate from there share a desire to take advantage of new opportunities.

regret coming for even one minute." Although Ahmed and Salwa had important jobs in their native land, between the two of them they earned the equivalent of about $60 each month. That was not nearly enough to raise their children, Hassan and Rana, and the new baby that was on the way back in 1995.

That year, Ahmed read in an Egyptian newspaper that the United States was holding a lottery. Winners would get a green card, a document that allows people from other countries to move to America to live and work legally. To his surprise, he won, and he excitedly (but nervously) made plans to travel to New York, where a distant cousin owned a street cart and sold quick, inexpensive lunches. It was hard work, and his cousin was always looking for reliable help.

Ahmed was worried about leaving his children and his pregnant wife, but he realized that this was the best chance he had to give his growing family a better life, so he set off.

Following in Others' Footsteps

The first significant wave of Middle Eastern immigrants began arriving in America in the late 19th century. As Ahmed would do more than a hundred years later, many came for the chance to earn more money and increase their standard of living. Some, however, came to escape religious **persecution** in the **Ottoman Empire**. Their identification cards and passports had been issued by the Ottomans, and confused US immigration officials used the terms "Turks," "Armenians," and "Syrians" interchangeably.

Most of these immigrants were single young men who practiced Christianity and didn't speak much English. Many dreamed of earning money in the United States and then returning home to find brides from

The Very Earliest Settlers

Although immigrants from the Middle East did not begin to arrive in the United States in any large numbers until the late 19th century, there are historical accounts of some arriving earlier.

In the mid-18th century, a royal **emissary** was sent from the region to explore the possibilities of establishing a Muslim presence in the New World. He was shipwrecked off the coast of Ocracoke Island, in the Outer Banks of North Carolina. He established a village there, and today a few Arabian horses, descendants of those he had traveled with, still roam the island.

In the mid-19th century, Hadj Ali, a Christian from Lebanon, came to America to work on the Camel Driver Experiment, a US Army project to establish a transportation route across the desert between Texas and California. The Americans pronounced his name "Hi Jolly," and he is still referred to in some history books that way and on this Arizona monument.

their own culture. Like other immigrant groups, a percentage of these Middle Easterners found that working as **peddlers** enabled them to earn a living and save money. They often sold embroidered linens and religious items they imported from their native lands. Married peddlers sometimes sold baked goods and candies made by their wives. (Ahmed points out that food carts like the one owned by his cousin have a lot in common with the peddlers' carts from that era, even though the modern version is equipped with a griddle, refrigerator, and other conveniences.)

Over time, this first wave of immigrants set enough money aside to start businesses. Often these were food related. Christine Sahadi Whelan's family owns the iconic Middle Eastern grocery store Sahadi's in downtown Brooklyn (see below). She explains, "Immigrants do what they know. In the case of my grandfather and his uncle, who came here from Lebanon, they knew food. Even today, if someone immigrates as an engineer or doctor, there are so many hoops to jump through in order to get licensed, it's just much easier to open a food business."

An American Classic from Lebanon

In 1895, Abrahim Sahadi, a Lebanese immigrant, opened A. Sahadi and Company in downtown Manhattan, where he sold groceries to the many families emigrating from the Ottoman Empire, which was then in decline. He imported foods and spices they would be familiar with and that they might miss from their homelands, like lentils, chickpeas, sumac, and grape leaves. In 1919, his nephew Wade came to the United States to join the business, and the store supported dozens of members of his extended family as they arrived in the city. In 1941, Wade, an opinionated man who regularly squabbled with his uncle over business decisions, struck out on his own, taking a supply of the stock on the shelves as his fair share and using them to open the Manhattan Sahadi Importing Company, just a block away from Abrahim's store.

He ultimately moved operations to Brooklyn, where the store became a beloved neighborhood institution, now run by his grandchildren Christine and Ron. The store is considered such an example of immigrant success and local character that it was named an American Classic by the James Beard Foundation.

New Waves of Immigration

By the 1920s there were about 250,000 Syrians, Lebanese, and Palestinians living in America. Not all, of course, started food or importing businesses. Many flocked to industrial cities like Detroit to work in manufacturing plants and factories.

By the 1950s immigrants from all over the Middle East, including Egypt, Yemen, and Jordan, had begun to settle in major cities across the entire United States. This new wave included greater numbers of **literate**, bilingual people seeking educational opportunities and professional careers. This led to what is sometimes called a brain drain, when a country's most highly skilled and educated people leave for other places. Meanwhile, the United States also saw an influx of European Jews who chose America rather than the fledgling nation of Israel, preferring the challenges of urban life to the challenges of living in a still-undeveloped desert land.

Amid the ongoing conflicts between **Arabs** and Jews who had settled

Jewish immigration to the United States

in the region, large numbers of **displaced** Palestinians came to the United States. By the 1960s, that group had a strong sense of ethnic and political awareness, and some experts think they helped spark the development of Arab American pride among older immigrants, as well as a new appreciation of Middle Eastern heritage. (That sense of pride helped sustain the other groups who subsequently immigrated to escape conflicts, including the long civil war that broke out in Lebanon in 1975, the war between Iraq and Iran in the 1980s, and the 1991 Gulf War.)

Ahmed appreciates his Egyptian culture, but during his first years in America it was hard to find time to do much besides work long hours, eat, sleep, and perform the prayer rituals that all Muslims are obligated to complete each day. Culture was far from the main thing on his mind.

Faithful Muslims are required to pray five times per day.

Luckily, because the meat he was serving at the food cart was halal, meaning that it had been prepared in accordance with Islamic law, he did not have to worry about finding meals he could eat. (Some people compare halal food with the kosher food eaten by observant Jews; both prohibit pork, for example, and both insist upon specific methods of butchering the animals.) "Praying and eating halal meals were the main ways I honored my culture," he said. "I know now there are many Middle Eastern groups to join and events to attend, but then, I just wanted to earn money as quickly as I could so that I could send for Salwa and the children to join me."

Text-Dependent Questions:

1. What was the Ottoman Empire?
2. What did married peddlers often sell?
3. What is halal food?

Research Project:

Ahmed was lucky to win the green card lottery, which is also known as the diversity visa lottery. Look up when (or if) the next lottery will be held and find out the rules and qualifications for entering.

APPETIZERS

It is a popular Middle Eastern tradition to serve a platter of assorted dips and appetizers called mezze. Some sources spell it meze. It is pronounced "meh-zeh," and the name comes from a Turkish word meaning "taste" or "flavor." Mezze can include a dizzying array of hot and cold dishes and can vary by specific region, but there are some that you are sure to find again and again.

Hummus is a smooth spread made from chickpeas and (usually) the rich sesame paste called tahini. The word "hummus" simply means "chickpea" in Arabic. It is among the best-known and well-loved of all Middle Eastern dishes, and cooks have been known to fight about who has the best recipe.

Lebanon later tried to register the word "hummus" to ban any other country from using that designation for their own chickpea dips (similar to the way cheese labeled Parmigiano Reggiano must be from Italy, and real Champagne must be from France). That attempt was unsuccessful, because authorities decided that hummus belonged to the entire region and that the whole Middle East should be proud of a dish whose popularity has spread throughout the world.

Another spread that is often included on the mezze platter is baba ghanoush. *It's popular, but it doesn't seem to ignite the quarreling that hummus does. To make baba ghanoush, a chef mashes together cooked eggplant, tahini, olive oil, garlic, and other spices. The Arabic word "baba" means "father," but there is some disagreement about what the word "ghanoush" means. Some food experts think it must be a family's surname, while others believe that it is derived from a word that means "pampered." Whether the dish was invented by a family named Ghanoush or whether it was created as a way to tempt the taste buds of a long-ago pampered papa, most people just know that it's delicious scooped onto a wedge of pita bread.*

APPETIZERS

If you order mezze at many restaurants, you may be puzzled to see what look like small, greenish cigars. These are stuffed grape leaves, also known as dolma or warak. To make this delicacy, the cook brines the large leaves found on grape vines (or buys them already brined in jars). The softened leaf is then used as a wrapper for various fillings, usually containing some mixture of rice, meat, and seasonings. "I would never have a party or family gathering without serving stuffed grape leaves," Christina Sahadi Whelan says. "Many people feel the same way. It's one of the dishes everyone who works in the store must know how to make, and we sell trays and trays of them every week."

Just as many Americans serve fancy cheese and crackers as a party appetizer, Middle Eastern hosts have their own cheese traditions. A mezze platter will sometimes contain a firm, salty cheese called Nabulsi, which originated in Nablus, Palestine.

Other popular cheeses include Syrian string cheese and labneh. The string cheese is made similar to the way mozzarella is made, and then flavored with mahlab *(ground seeds from the St. Lucy's cherry).*

Labneh is made from thick yogurt and sometimes rolled into balls, which are then coated in sesame seeds, crushed nuts, chili flakes, and other seasonings.

Settling In

Ahmed lived with his cousin when he first arrived in America, sleeping on an inflatable mattress in the living room of an apartment in Queens, a borough of New York City that attracts immigrants from all over the world. Three other men—immigrants from the same Egyptian town—shared the tiny apartment.

Many immigrants share apartments with family, friends, or coworkers to save money on rent, and often they must settle in poor or rundown neighborhoods. Such crowded living spaces can be unsafe, because having a lot of appliances, lamps, and fans plugged into extension cords is a fire hazard. When it's cold, residents

Words to Understand

countrymen people who are all from the same country or region

diverse composed of many different elements or types of things

ethnic enclave a place where minority communities maintain ways of life separate from those of the larger communities surrounding them

sister cities places in geographically and politically distinct areas that formally agree to promote cultural and business ties

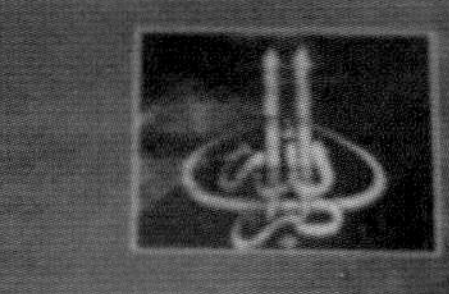

English translations of the Muslim holy book, the Qur'an, are sold on the streets of Jackson Heights, Queens, in New York City.

might huddle around a space heater or open oven, posing even more danger of fire. At Ahmed's cousin's apartment, the bathroom plumbing often stopped working, and because there weren't enough closets for all of the roommates, their clothing and other belongings was piled up on chairs and on the floor.

Ahmed lived in the crowded apartment for three long years, saving every penny he could, before he was finally able to afford to send for Salwa, Hassan, Rana, and the youngest member of the family, Marwa—the baby Salwa had given birth to just a few months after Ahmed won the green card lottery and traveled to America. Salwa was two-and-a-half years old and had never even met her father when she boarded a plane to join him, spending much of the 12-hour journey either sleeping or

Immigrants hope to qualify for the US permanent resident, or green card.

nestled in Salwa's lap to look out the window with wide eyes. No one in the family had ever been on a plane before, but their fear and excitement was nothing compared to the fear and excitement they each felt about settling into a new home.

Ahmed had found them a two-bedroom apartment in a Queens neighborhood called Astoria. The rent was higher than he would have liked, but it was a safe area, and best of all, it had a street known as Little Egypt, where Salwa could shop for familiar groceries and where she might meet other women to become friends with. (Queens is the most **diverse** borough of New York City and one of the most diverse places in the entire United States. Almost half of Queens residents hail from another country. One reporter walked along a three-block stretch—from 83rd St. to 86th St. in a neighborhood called Jackson Heights—and he met immigrants from 51 different countries, speaking 21 different languages!)

"Even though money was tight, I felt like a rich man as soon as I had my family with me," Ahmed recalls. After two more years, with Salwa watching every penny she spent on groceries and clothes for the growing children, he had saved enough to get his own cart, which he set up each day a few blocks from his cousin's.

Settling into the Suburbs

While it is always hard to settle into a new home, immigrants who choose large cities can usually at least find others who speak their language and understand their struggles. Frederique Boudouani, who emigrated from Algeria, took a chance when he fell in love with his partner, a native of the Midwest whom he met while both were in college in Boston. The two decided to move to Iowa, where there happened to be a town named after a 19th-century Algerian Muslim.

Elkader is home to only about 1,500 people and is surrounded by corn fields. Thanks to Boudouani, it is now also home to an Algerian restaurant. While the restaurant looks like a regular American diner, an Algerian flag hangs on the wall next to the Stars and Stripes, and a picture of Emir Abd el-Kader, famed for leading a resistance against French colonial forces, is displayed prominently. Elkader's founders had read reports of his bravery and in 1836 decided to name their new town after him.

In the 1980s the Algerian Embassy invited Elkader to join a **sister cities** program and paired it with Mascara, Algeria. The mayor, who had traveled to Mascara when the town joined the program, loved to discuss the town's name and its Algerian connection; he welcomed Boudouani warmly and helped him go about getting the licenses and permissions needed to open a business. (The mayor especially appreciated the fact that

Welcome to Elkader!

the restaurant, which serves traditional Algerian dishes, drew visitors to Elkader who might not otherwise come.)

Boudouani is happy to tell people about his native country, but says that Elkader is home now!

Ethnic Enclaves

Elkader is a welcoming place, and Boudouani's restaurant is popular, but the town could hardly be called an **ethnic enclave**. Social scientists describe an enclave as a place where minority communities maintain ways of life separate from those of the larger communities surrounding them. Most large cities have a so-called Chinatown, for example, where

The main street of Elkader, Iowa, where residents have used the town's Arab-influenced name to create a dialogue with an Algerian sister city.

immigrants from Asia have settled to live, shop, and eat, and where tourists flock for more authentic Asian food than they can find in their own neighborhoods.

Ethnic enclaves can help new immigrants feel more comfortable in their adopted country because people usually have a natural desire to stay in their comfort zones.

Living in Little Egypt helped Salwa feel a lot more comfortable. Because other women covered their hair for modesty, just as she did, people did not stare or point at her traditional headscarf, which extended down over her neck and shoulders. Although she had learned some English in school as a young girl, she had forgotten most of it. Strolling down the few blocks of Astoria's Steinway Street that made up Little Egypt, she enjoyed peering in shop windows filled with products she recognized

In a part of Queens that is home to many immigrants, some areas have a concentration of people from Arabic places.

and chatting in Arabic with the clerks and other shoppers. She could buy music CDs with Egyptian singers, rent Arabic-language movies, and bring home Egyptian newspapers so that Ahmed could read about current events going on in the Middle East.

Economists point out that besides being cultural comfort zones, ethnic enclaves serve as places where immigrant entrepreneurs can start businesses that cater to the specific tastes and needs of their communities and provide jobs for their **countrymen**.

Jewish Delis

Wherever they settled, be it Israel or the United States, the Jews of Europe (especially Germany) bought a tasty tradition of smoking and pickling meats with them. Some opened delicatessens (or delis), serving the savory corned beef or spicy pastrami they remembered from their homelands.

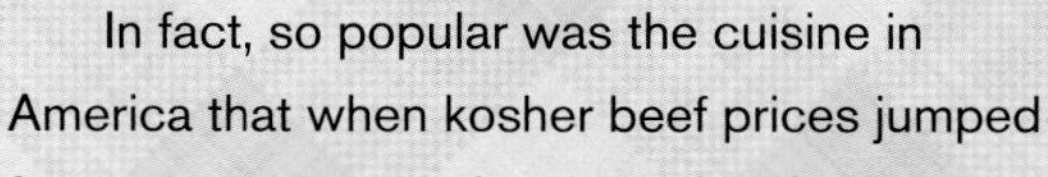

In fact, so popular was the cuisine in America that when kosher beef prices jumped from 12 to 18 cents in 1902, riots broke out in Jewish enclaves throughout the Northeast before prices settled back down.

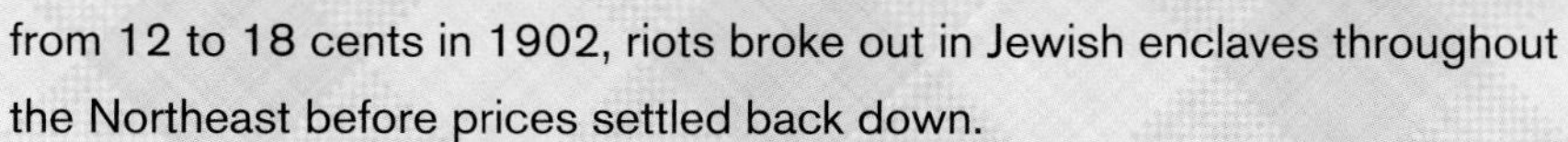

Over subsequent decades, more and more immigrants opened delis, staying connected to their heritage, earning a living, and helping introduce non-Jews to Jewish culture. In the 1930s, at the peak, there were some 1,500 delis in New York City alone. Today, while you can still find kosher and kosher-style delis throughout the country, their numbers have greatly diminished. Most people now know that although it's delicious, it's pretty unhealthy to eat salty, fatty meat all the time!

New York City is not the only metropolitan area with Middle Eastern enclaves, of course. In Los Angeles, California, you can find Little Persia. It's sometimes called Tehrangeles, a mash-up of Los Angeles and Tehran (the capital city of Iran). The area was formed after the 1979 Iranian revolution, when those seeking to escape their country's authoritarian and repressive regime fled to America. Los Angeles now has the highest number of Persians living outside of Iran, and the enclave caters to them with dessert shops that sell saffron ice cream, casual kebob stands, and upscale restaurants for multicourse Iranian feasts.

Sometimes, ethnic enclaves grow smaller or disappear over time, as immigrants join the mainstream or newer immigrant groups from other

Iranian-Americans and their neighbors celebrate the annual Norooz Festival with a parade in Los Angeles.

countries arrive. New York City once had an area known as Little Syria, where Abrahim Sahadi got his start. The community thrived from the 1880s to the 1940s, with multiple coffee houses and kebob shops. Today, the only buildings remaining from the once-bustling enclave are a church, an apartment building, and a community center.

Enclaves of ultra-religious Jews live in many major cities in America and Europe. Some of these are Chasidim, members of a sect founded in 18th-century Poland. Chasidim wear special clothing and hats that set them apart from their non-religious neighbors, and they speak and read mainly Yiddish, rather than English. Because they are forbidden to drive on the Sabbath, their enclaves always include places of worship that can be reached on foot. Restaurants and stores sell foods that comply with kosher dietary laws, which prohibit eating pork and shellfish and forbid mixing meat and dairy products in the same meal.

Text-Dependent Questions:

1. What percentage of residents in the New York City borough of Queens hails from another country?
2. How did the town of Elkader, Iowa, get its name?
3. What Middle Eastern nation has a large population in Los Angeles?

Research Project:

Most metropolitan areas have ethnic enclaves of some type. Look up the ones close to where you live. Write out the plan for a trip there. What shops will you visit? Where will you eat?

FIRST COURSE

In Israel, many people eat a salad with each and every meal. That even includes breakfast! Some people say that's because all the vegetables grown there are so fresh and full of flavor. Even though it's a dry land, Israelis have developed modern and efficient methods of agriculture, and Israel is generally near the top of the list on surveys of average fruit and vegetable consumption per person.

Salads are served at home, restaurants, food stands, and shopping mall food courts, and the usual mixture includes finely chopped tomatoes, cucumbers, peppers, fresh lemon juice, olive oil, and a little salt and pepper.

If you go to a Jewish deli or a Middle Eastern restaurant in America, you'll probably see this colorful, finely chopped blend labeled Israeli salad. Interestingly enough, that's not what they call it in Israel. There it's generally known as salat katzutz *(chopped salad) or* salat aravi *(Arab salad).*

FIRST COURSE

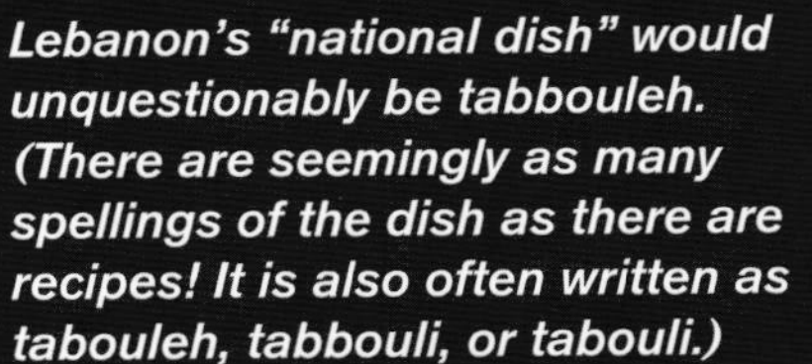

Tabbouleh is a salad made of lots of finely chopped parsley, mint, onion, and bulgur (a kind of wheat that has been cracked and partially cooked), all tossed together with olive oil and lemon juice. Cooks frequently put their own spin on it—adding tomatoes, cucumbers, and garlic or leaving out the mint, but everyone agrees that it wouldn't be tabbouleh without the parsley and bulgur.

Tabbouleh's name comes from the Arabic word tabil, *which can mean either "seasoning" or "dip." Food historians think that the dish originated in the Levant, an old geographic term referring to Syria, Lebanon, and Palestine. They have specifically traced its beginnings to the mountains bordering Lebanon and Syria, but explain that it quickly spread throughout the region because of the bustling commercial trade there.*

Americanized versions feature mainly bulgur, with some parsley or mint sprinkled in for color. However, Lebanese chefs believe the key to an authentic tabbouleh is lots and lots of the green stuff.

3 Connecting

Some experts think that living in an ethnic enclave, like Ahmed and his family do, will slow down the process of **assimilation**, or becoming truly American. That wasn't the case with the Maloof family. They loved their apartment and their neighbors in Little Egypt, but they also moved comfortably in other environments after a while.

Hassan, Rana, and Marwa attended public schools in Queens that attracted large numbers of recently arrived immigrants—all learning about their new country together, making friends, and helping each other out. Hassan and Rana were old enough to remember their schools in Egypt and agree that they like their new ones better. Back in their homeland, boys and girls studied separately, and teachers were so strict that they often yelled—and sometimes even hit students who misbehaved

Words to Understand

assimilation the process of taking something and making it a true part of the thing it has joined

franchise establishments with the right to sell a larger company's goods or services in a particular spot

Students in the United States wearing the hijab, a tradtional head covering worn by women in the Islamic faith.

with a thick wooden paddle. Classes could be overcrowded and hot. In Queens, boys and girls studied together in spacious classrooms with plenty of supplies, and teachers hardly ever yelled.

Encouraged by her children's success, Salwa began taking English classes for adult immigrants. Held at a local college, the classes also taught her more about American customs and traditions. The week of Thanksgiving the teacher brought in an enormous turkey, and each student contributed a dish from their native country. Salwa made *kobeba*, a type of beef turnover that can be found, in regional variations, all over the Middle East. In Lebanon, for example, *kibbe*, as it's called, is almost as beloved as tabbouleh.

A Zest for Life

"Of course I love to serve kibbe, and like most Lebanese cooks, I pride myself on my recipe," Lorraine Harik says. "So when my son was growing up and wanted to eat something typically American, I'd make a big meatloaf. But while American-born cooks might use torn-up pieces of white bread or dried bread crumbs, my meat loaf had bulgur in it and was seasoned like kibbe."

Lorraine was especially fond of using a blend of herbs called *za'atar*, which is popular throughout the Middle East. The exact ingredients vary, depending on the country, but in Lebanon the mixture always includes plenty of sumac, made by drying the fruit of a particular shrub and grinding it into powder. (In Jordan, cardamom is added, while Syrians prefer cumin.) Her son, Alexander, considered *za'atar* a big part of his childhood (the family even sprinkled it on popcorn while they were watching movies), and as an adult he wanted to recreate some of the Lebanese dishes Lorraine had served when he was young. He also wanted to make *manoushe*, flatbread spread with *za'atar* and sold from street carts all over Lebanon. (It's such a popular snack food that it invites comparisons to another worldwide favorite; it's often called Lebanese pizza.) No *za'atar* he could buy tasted as good to him as the one his mother had blended with wild thyme, sesame seeds, and sumac. He convinced Lorraine to quit her job to help him launch a company: Zesty Z.

"Think about it," he says. "Twenty years ago you didn't see hummus or Greek yogurt being eaten on a daily basis here in America, but today those foods can be found in every supermarket. I hope 20 years from now it will be the same for *za'atar*."

Manoushe covered with za'atar *is a flatbread called Lebanese pizza.*

In Reality

If you're a fan of reality television, you might be familiar with Jay Hajj, the chef-owner of Mike's City Diner in Boston (right). Hajj appears frequently on Food Network shows like *Diners, Drive-Ins and Dives* and *Guy's Grocery Games*. But way before he discovered he was a natural behind the stove and in front of the camera, he was a boy in war-torn Beirut, "caught quite literally in the crossfire of the Lebanese Civil War," as he wrote in his cookbook-memoir *From Beirut to Boston*.

"The foods we ate to survive were Lebanese versions of the time-honored cuisine of the Arab and Middle Eastern worlds," he wrote. "Beans. Rice. Lamb on occasion. Plenty of fresh and colorful fruits and vegetables such as figs, lemons, and pomegranates. And the beautiful, aromatic spices of the Middle East and Mediterranean, including allspice, cinnamon, and Aleppo pepper."

The family fled to the United States when Hajj was eight years old, and by 13 he was working in local restaurants, marveling at the new dishes and flavors available to him in his adopted home. Now, the menu at Mike's City Diner reflects all of those influences. "My path was flavored by the comfort-food cuisine of two different cities and two different cultures, then woven together in a uniquely American tapestry," he wrote.

One year, the Food Network even named his Pilgrim sandwich—a towering mass of turkey, stuffing, and cranberry sauce—as one of the Five Best Thanksgiving Meals in America.

Healthy and Halal

Thanks to venders like Ahmed, hundreds of American office workers every day get to see what halal food is like. For $6 his customers get to choose seasoned chicken or lamb seared on a grill and served over rice, along with a small salad and a delicious white sauce some of them joke that they are addicted to. (Most vendors keep the exact recipe a secret but say it contains caraway, sumac, cardamom, and turmeric.)

It isn't always easy. Ahmed was required to take a health and safety class from the city and was grateful that it was offered in Arabic. He had to apply for a food vendor license and take his cart in to be inspected by the city's health department regularly. Those things cost money he could not always afford, but the worst part was being away from his family for long hours. He woke at 5 each morning to get his cart from the garage where he pays to store it, push it to the portion of sidewalk he has staked out on a busy section of Lexington Avenue, hook up the massive propane

Selling halal food

tank that powers the grill, and begin preparing the food a halal grocer delivers to him each day.

The American Dream

Ahmed dreams of being as successful one day as Muhammed Aboue-lenein, Ahmed Elsaka, and Abdelbaset Elsayed, three Egyptian food vendors who set up a hot dog cart on West 53rd Street and Sixth Avenue in New York City back in 1990. Their hot dogs sold well to tourists and office workers, but they realized that the city's devoutly Muslim cab drivers, who also needed inexpensive, tasty lunches, would not eat hot dogs containing pork.

Busy food carts that sell popular halal food on the street also stock American favorites such as hot dogs.

They began serving halal chicken and lamb over rice (and the now-famous white sauce), and the idea exploded. Soon similar carts were parked all over the city. Still, their fans could always spot carts that belonged to the trio because of their distinctive red-and-yellow lettering and their registered brand name: the Halal Guys.

Now the Halal Guys have not only carts but two actual restaurants in New York City, and **franchises** are popping up in places like Las Vegas, Washington, Atlanta, Houston, and Chicago, as well as Canada, Malaysia, and the Philippines.

Text-Dependent Questions:

1. Does living in an ethnic enclave always slow the process of assimilation?
2. How is sumac made?
3. Why couldn't Muslim cab drivers eat hot dogs from a New York City food cart?

Research Project:

Pretend you are a new immigrant who wants to operate a food cart in New York City. Look up the requirements. How much money would you need to get started? Write down your business plan.

SECOND COURSE

Across the Middle East it is not uncommon for meals to include a wide variety of meats and vegetables, rather than just the one main dish common in American households.

A meal could feature kebobs as the main attraction: cubes of chicken, beef, or lamb seasoned and then grilled on long skewers. (Those who follow halal traditions will never serve pork.) Food historians think the practice of cooking meat on a skewer might date back to prehistoric times, when early humans discovered the uses of fire.

Kebobs are so popular in Iran that some people consider them the national dish. In Israel, kebobs are the dish of choice for grilling on national holidays. In Egypt, shish taouk, *chicken skewers marinated in olive oil and spices, is a favorite.*

Shawarma is popular everywhere in the former Ottoman Empire. The dish got its name from the Turkish word çevirme, which means "turning." To make shawarma, you need a large revolving rotisserie, turning near an open flame or other heat source. As the meat turns, slivers are shaved off and served on platters or tucked into sandwiches.

Not every Middle Eastern meal uses meat as a protein source. Among the best-known and popular dishes to come out of the region is falafel, savory little balls or patties made of ground chickpeas that are fried and then enjoyed on their own or stuffed into pita. As with hummus, the dish's origin is a source of some dispute among Arabs and Israelis. One often-seen tourist postcard pictures falafel with the caption "Israel's National Snack," and many Israelis would like to consider the chickpea fritters uniquely theirs. Palestinians assert, on the other hand, that they were the ones who discovered how delicious mashed-up and fried chickpeas could be.

4 Reaching Back

Even when an immigrant assimilates, certain cultural touchstones remain. "For us that would definitely include hospitality," Lorraine Harik explains. "Every Middle Eastern culture stresses how important it is to welcome guests and feed them well." Some sociologists think that **ethos** of hospitality dates back to Bedouin **nomads**, who traveled through the desert and often called upon the hospitality of those they encountered to survive attacks by enemies, hunger, and thirst. Gradually, the custom of caring for the stranger spread to other Arab groups, including those living non-nomadic lives in villages.

It is therefore not unusual for a holiday dinner to include dozens of friends and relatives. Such joyful events provide a way for immigrants—even the most assimilated—to remain connected to their culture and customs.

Words to Understand

ethos the characteristic spirit of a culture, era, or community

nomad a member of a group that has no fixed home but instead wanders from place to place

hijab head coverings worn by Muslim women

Dressing in costume is part of the Jewish holiday of Purim, here celebrated in Israel. Similar scenes are found among Jewish immigrant populations.

Celebrate!

One of the most joyful and food-filled days of the year for the world's Muslims is Eid al-Fitr. That day marks the end of the holy month of Ramadan, when devout Muslims refrain from eating and drinking from dawn to dusk each day. Fasting for hours each day for an entire month is a challenge, so everyone looks forward to the Eid al-Fitr feast, which always includes special sweets and delicacies.

From the 1930s to the 1960s, holding large community festivals featuring music performances, dance, and traditional foods was a popular way to keep Arab culture alive and pass it on to a younger generation. These

The Eid al-Fitr fast is often broken with a communal meal, such as this gathering in Madrid, Spain.

Ramadan and Football

Dearborn is a town in Michigan where more than 30 percent of the residents are Arab Americans. Some classes are taught in both English and Arabic in Dearborn's public schools, women in hijab are a common sight, and the town has long had council members and other important officials of Arab descent. The Dearborn McDonald's even serves halal meat! (Other restaurants focus on Middle East food, such as the one below.)

So when the start of football season coincided with Ramadan one year, the coach was worried. In middle-class suburban school districts like Dearborn's, football is an important facet of life, but he wondered how his team—90 percent of whom were Muslim—would fare practicing in the heat without having eaten for hours. The solution? Simply delay practice until 11 p.m., allowing players to break their fast at sunset, drink plenty of water and eat a light meal, practice in the cool darkness, and eat a substantial meal before sunrise.

In 2011, a filmmaker named Rashid Ghazi was so moved by the story that he made a documentary about the team called *Fordson: Faith, Fasting, Football.* "There is nothing more American than high school football," Ghazi once told a reporter. "It just so happens that this all-American story is set in an area with hijabs, mosques, and baklava rather than baseball caps, churches and apple pie."

were called *mahrajanat* and people looked forward to them all year long. In the 1970s, as the economy worsened, it became harder for communities to organize such extravagant events and *mahrajanat* fell out of favor. Some cities are trying to revive the custom though, so keep your eyes open for a *mahrajan* in your area.

For Israelis and American Jews alike, holidays mean eating certain foods. On Passover, which celebrates the Jewish people's liberation from slavery in ancient Egypt, crispy cracker-like matzo is eaten instead of bread, because tradition has it that the slaves left in such a rush that their dough didn't even have time to rise. During the winter festival of Hanukah, it's customary to eat foods fried in oil. In America, that usually means savory potato pancakes called latkes, while in Israel they are partial to sweet, deep-fried jelly doughnuts known as *sufganiyot*.

Giving Back

Like many immigrant groups, people from the Middle East stay connected to their homelands by sending money to friends and family who have remained behind or by giving to charities or causes important there. In a survey conducted by *Forbes* magazine, two-thirds of Middle Eastern philanthropists said they were motivated by their faith to give, and the vast majority wanted to stay anonymous, preferring to not publicize their acts of generosity.

Many philanthropists are devoted to causes that will improve education and quality of life in their native lands. In 2015, for example, the founder and chairman of a bank in Dubai gave a jaw-dropping $1.1 billion to fund scholarships for underprivileged students in the United Arab Emirates.

It is often said that the pioneers who founded the modern nation of

Israel made the desert bloom. Some of that greenery came courtesy of the Jewish National Fund (JNF), an organization that was founded in 1901 to help establish a new Jewish homeland. Even before Israel was officially established, the JNF began planting trees in the region, and they later had a wildly successful idea: If a Jew living anywhere in the world gave a small donation, a tree would be planted specifically in their honor (or in memory of a loved one who had died). By 2001, its 100-year anniversary, the JNF had arranged for more than 250 million trees, and for many American Jews, planting a tree in Israel remains a cultural and charitable touchstone.

Visitors to Israel, or people donating money to help that country, often plant a tree there as a symbol of their connection to the land.

Join the Club

In the 1970s and 1980s, as people began to take growing pride in their Arab roots, organizations started to spring up, including the National Arab American Association and the Arab American Institute. These groups helped spread a positive and wholesome view of the culture to those who might never have encountered anyone of Arab descent. They also helped protect the rights of Arab immigrants.

That function became especially important after the terrorist attacks of September 11, 2001. In the aftermath of that terrible day, Middle Easterners were subjected to hate crimes, bigotry, discrimination, and racial profiling.

Sadly, the choice by an Islamic woman to wear traditional clothing has led to some ignorant and bigoted attacks and statements.

Inside the Arab American Association

Salwa became afraid to wear her headscarf in public, and Hassan came home from school in tears one day because a classmate, herself an immigrant from China, had called him a terrorist. Ahmed had the most troubling encounter. One day, as he wearily maneuvered his food cart into position on the sidewalk, a well-dressed man pulled his car to the curb. Ahmed assumed he intended to enter a nearby office building and politely mentioned to him that the spot he had chosen was, in fact, in a no-parking zone and that he risked incurring an expensive fine. Without saying a word, the man grasped him by the collar and punched him directly in the face. Shocked, Ahmed watched as the blood pouring out of his nose dripped onto his shirt. Unsure of how to react, he pushed the man away, and both landed clumsily on the sidewalk. Ahmed was relieved when he looked up and saw two police officers fast approaching. That relief turned to confusion when one officer carefully helped the man up while the other yanked Ahmed roughly to his feet and forced a pair of handcuffs on his wrists.

Ahmed remembered that a few weeks before he had picked up a card at the library advertising the services of an Arab American advocacy group, and one panicky call later, a young lawyer appeared at the precinct house and had Ahmed released. Severely shaken, he considered returning with his family to Egypt. "I decided this is my home though," he says. "I'm proud to be an American now, and even when things get rough or people are unwelcoming, that doesn't change the fact that this is my home." "Besides," he concludes, "my customers have been very supportive. They count on me to feed them each day, and I'm happy to do it."

People from the Middle East join diverse populations around the world.

Ahmed not only provides his customers with a nourishing lunch. He provides them with a window into the immigrant experience and a different way of life. Many of them consider him a good friend and say that knowing him has allowed them to see just how much newcomers contribute to the country. His bright, hardworking children are sure to contribute as well in the years to come. He and others like him are proof that when borders are crossed and hearts are opened, everyone can benefit.

Text-Dependent Questions:

1. What is a nomad?
2. When does Eid al-Fitr occur?
3. What happened on 9/11?

Research Project:

Dearborn is an unusual town. Look up its history and write a paragraph about how it came to be a hub for Muslim immigrants.

DESSERT

A hospitable Middle Eastern family will usually offer a sweet treat at the end of a meal. Some of these delicacies are also shared with tea for visitors or as snacks for hungry children.

Umm ali, *sometimes described as Egyptian bread pudding is made of flaky phyllo dough, cream, and nuts, and is widely enjoyed throughout Egypt.*

Many Middle Easterners look forward to cooking and eating qatayef, *which are sometimes called Arabic pancakes, during Ramadan. Batter is poured on a hot pan or griddle and then filled with sweet cheese or nuts, folded, and then deep-fried or baked.*

In addition to baked goods, the Middle East is known for a variety of traditional candies. Some of them have unexpected ingredients, like the sesame seeds in halvah. *A crumbly confection, halvah is made from the sesame paste known as tahini (pictured below mixed with a syrup of molten sugar. Both remain popular with Middle Eastern immigrants with fond childhood memories of eating sesame cookies, pistachio halvah, and tahini mixed with date honey.*

COFFEE OR TEA?

Coffee was first discovered as a drink in the ninth century in Ethiopia. Word spread, and soon farmers on the Arabian Peninsula began cultivating coffee plants. The drink became popular in Yemen, Egypt, Syria, and elsewhere, and today *qahwa*, as it's known in Arabic, is an important part of culture throughout the Middle East.

Different countries in the Middle East have different ways of preparing and serving coffee. In Egypt, it is served in a small cup with a frothy layer of foam on top, while in Lebanon it is poured into larger cups with no foam. Sometimes it is infused with cardamom, cinnamon, cloves, saffron, or ginger, to give it subtle added flavor. No matter how it is prepared, coffee is vital to Middle Eastern life.

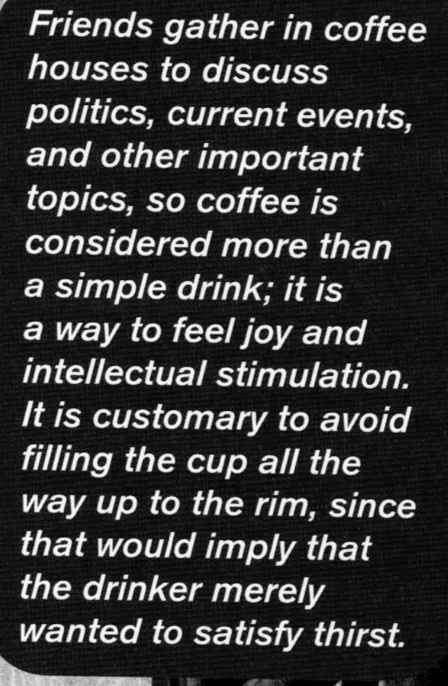

Friends gather in coffee houses to discuss politics, current events, and other important topics, so coffee is considered more than a simple drink; it is a way to feel joy and intellectual stimulation. It is customary to avoid filling the cup all the way up to the rim, since that would imply that the drinker merely wanted to satisfy thirst.

In the early 19th century, as the British Empire was growing, tea caught on in some Middle Eastern countries, like Egypt and Iran. It is still a popular alternative to coffee in parts of the region and is often made with mint.

RECIPES

Super-Simple Hummus

Here's a quick and easy version of the popular dish. You might be tempted to eat it by the spoonful, but it's better as a dip for veggies, crackers, or wedges of pita. This recipe will make about 1½ cups.

Ingredients:

1 (15 oz.) can chickpeas, drained and rinsed
2 to 4 Tbsp water
2 Tbsp olive oil
1 Tbsp lemon juice
1 garlic clove, minced
½ tsp ground cumin
½ tsp salt

Preparation:

1. Add the chickpeas, 2 tablespoons of the water, the olive oil, lemon juice, garlic, cumin, and salt to a food processor or strong blender. Process until smooth and creamy. If needed, add additional water to thin out the hummus.
2. Store covered in the refrigerator.

Tabbouleh

This colorful, healthy salad would be perfect to take to a summer picnic or potluck. (This recipe will make enough for a big bowl to share with friends.) You can find bulgur in most supermarkets, but if not, it can also be purchased in health food stores.

Ingredients:

- *1 cup bulgur*
- *3 tomatoes, chopped (squeeze as many of the seeds out as you can before chopping)*
- *2 cucumbers, peeled and chopped*
- *3 scallions, chopped*
- *3 cloves garlic, minced*
- *1 cup chopped fresh parsley (measure after chopping)*
- *1/3 cup fresh mint leaves, chopped*
- *2 tsp salt*
- *1/2 cup lemon juice*
- *2/3 cup olive oil*

Preparation:

Place bulgur in a bowl and cover it with 2 cups boiling water. Soak for 30 minutes; drain and squeeze out extra water.
In a mixing bowl, combine the bulgur, tomatoes, cucumbers, scallions, garlic, parsley, mint, salt, lemon juice, and olive oil. Toss and refrigerate for a few minutes before serving.

Find Out More

Film

Take a wide-ranging look at Israeli food and its origins with award-winning chef Michael Solomonov in the 2016 documentary *In Search of Israeli Cuisine*.

Books

Bayoumi, Moustafa. ***How Does It Feel to Be a Problem: Being Young and Arab in America.*** New York: Penguin Books, 2008.

Bishara, Rawia. ***Olives, Lemons & Za'atar: The Best Middle Eastern Home Cooking.*** London: Kyle Books, 2014.

Iyer, Rukmini. ***Middle Eastern Kitchen: Authentic Dishes from the Middle East.*** Bath, UK: Parragon Books, 2016.

Websites

https://www.cia.gov/library/publications/the-world-factbook/
Read a fact-filled guide to the geography, history, and culture of every country in the Middle East.

https://bethanykehdy.com/
This culture and recipe blog is written by a Lebanese-American cook eager to share the tastes and joys of Middle Eastern food and help people understand its depth and complexity.

www.arabamericanmuseum.org/
Browse the virtual exhibits and learn all about the history and culture of Arabs in America.

Series Glossary of Key Terms

acclimate to get used to something

assimilate become part of a different society, country, or group

bigotry treating the members of a racial or ethnic group with hatred and intolerance

culinary having to do with the preparing of food

diaspora a group of people who live outside the area in which they had lived for a long time or in which their ancestors lived

emigrate leave one's home country to live in another country

exodus a mass departure of people from one place to another

first-generation American someone born in the United States whose parents were foreign-born

immigrants those who enter another country intending to stay permanently

naturalize to gain citizenship, with its rights and privileges

oppression a system of forcing people to follow rules or a system that restricts freedoms

presentation in this series, the style in which food is plated and served

Index

Photo Credits

Alamy Stock: Vesapasian 23; Ira Berger 28. Dreamstime.com: Meunierd 8; Jennifer Russell 16; Gaurav Masand 18; Annpustynnikova 19T; David Cabrera Navarro 19B; Sergevpsb 20T; Alexander Mychko 20B; Sivtlana Tereschencko 21; Leerobin 24; Zhukovsky 20; Paul Brighton 34; Travelling-light 35, 61; Rawpixelimages 37; Farbled 39; Rafael Ben Ari 42; Igor Skryagin 44; Erkan Kurt 45T; Jennifer Barrow 45B; Mazor 47; Demidoff 48; James R. Martin 49; Michelle and Tom Grimm 51; Odua 54; Cristalyn Pastrana 56T; Paul Cowan 56B; Kornelijia 57T; Nataliya Arzamasova 57B; Olga Vasileyva 58; Essentialimagemedia 59T; Muhammad Yasin Irik 59B; Elena Elisseva 60. MikeCityDiner.com: 40. Shutterstock: Zurijeta 7, 11; Beto Rodrigues 30; Ron Zmiri 33; ZouZou 52. Wikimedia CC: Jeremy Butler 13; Kevin Schuchmann 27; Gila Brand 32.

Author Bio

Mari Rich was educated at Lehman College, part of the public City University of New York. As a writer and editor, she has had many years of experience in the fields of university communications and reference publishing, most notably with the highly regarded periodical Current Biography, aimed at high school and college readers. She also edited and wrote for *World Authors, Leaders of the Information Age,* and *Nobel Laureates*. Currently, she spends much of her time writing about engineers and engineering.